Crofting People and Politics

Crofting People and Politics

FIVE DECADES OF THE CROFTERS COMMISSION

CROFTERS COMMISSION

UGHDARRAS NAN CROITEARAN
50 YEARS SUPPORTING CROFTING

1955/2005

ARGYLL ❖ PUBLISHING

© 2005 Crofters Commission

Argyll Publishing
Glendaruel
Argyll PA22 3AE
Scotland
www.argyllpublishing.com

Crofters Commission
Castle Wynd
Inverness IV2 3EQ
tel 01463 663450
www.crofterscommission.org.uk

British Library Cataloguing-in-Publication Data.
A catalogue record for this book is available from the
British Library.

ISBN 1 902831 91 8

Origination: Cordfall Ltd, Glasgow

Printing: Bell & Bain Ltd, Glasgow

Croft at Ballantrusal, Lewis

Melbost Crofts, Lewis

Contents

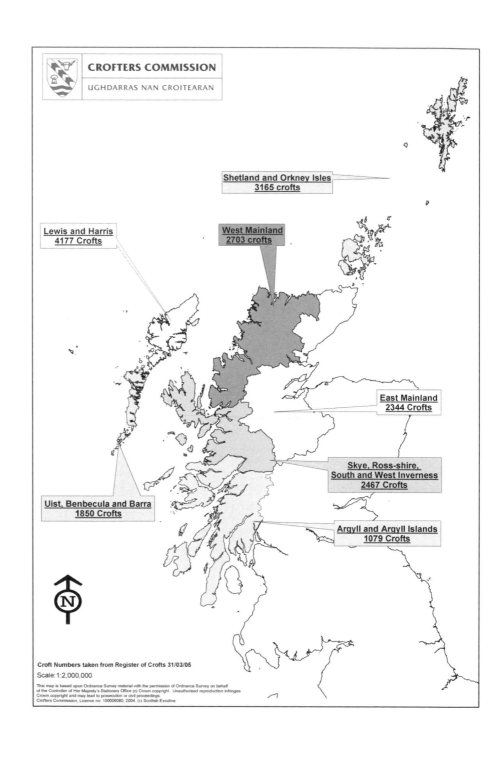

CROFTERS COMMISSION

UGHDARRAS NAN CROITEARAN

Shetland and Orkney Isles
3165 crofts

Lewis and Harris
4177 Crofts

West Mainland
2703 crofts

East Mainland
2344 Crofts

Skye, Ross-shire,
South and West Inverness
2467 Crofts

Uist, Benbecula and Barra
1850 Crofts

Argyll and Argyll Islands
1079 Crofts

N

Croft Numbers taken from Register of Crofts 31/03/05

Scale:1:2,000,000

This map is based upon Ordnance Survey material with the permission of Ordnance Survey on behalf
of the Controller of Her Majesty's Stationery Office (c) Crown copyright. Unauthorised reproduction infringes
Crown copyright and may lead to prosecution or civil proceedings.
Crofters Commission, Licence no: 100008080, 2004. (c) Scottish Excutive

FOREWORD

Rhona Brankin
Deputy Minister
for Environment and Rural Development

Rhona Brankin

Fifty years ago the Crofters Commission was established, but its story began long before in the plight of ordinary people of the Highlands and Islands.

The first witness to appear before the Napier Commission in 1883 was a Skye crofter, who said that he could not give evidence as to the distress of his people until he was given an assurance that he and his family would not be evicted. Lord Napier won that assurance from the estate for him.

The 1886 Crofting Act, which built on the Napier Commission's findings, gave every crofter that same assurance – security of tenure.

In the 120 years that have passed since, every government has upheld this guarantee, and the Scottish Executive will be no different. Indeed the Scottish Executive and Parliament have already gone further. We gave to crofting communities alone an unprecedented right to buy their land, whether or not it was for sale, as long as it was in the public interest. It underlined our view that crofting communities are integral to any meaningful programme of land reform.

We relocated from Edinburgh to Tiree, the jobs of those civil servants who processed applications for crofter building grants and loans. We believed they should no longer be in the heart of the capital but should be in one of our remoter crofting communities – a move that wouldn't even have been considered just ten years ago.

In addition we are proposing to allow the creation of new crofts, not necessarily adjacent to existing croftland. We will also examine the potential for forest crofts carved out of the 667,000 hectar es of forests and other land owned by Scottish Ministers and managed by Forestry

Commission Scotland. This could prove one of most exciting developments of them all and could go a long way to helping the chronic shortage of affordable housing in rural areas, particularly for the young.

We need to encourage new people into crofting including those who have had no earlier ties with the particular area, but have energy and enterprise. We will, however, never forget those whose attachment to their land goes back through generations. They are and will remain crofting's lifeblood.

We cannot visualise a Scotland without crofting and crofters, new and old. They have a vital role to play in shaping the new Scotland. They can increasingly provide a bridge between the too often opposing interests of conservation and development, and help us find the right balance that will allow the Highlands and Islands continue to grow economically without prejudicing our unrivalled natural environment.

I have lived most of my adult life in the crofting counties and have long recognised crofting as the social cornerstone of the Highlands and Islands, sustaining the Gaelic culture through long dark days. But increasingly crofting is also being recognised as a sustainable system of land management. Crofts were never just small farms. Indeed because of the marginal nature of much of the land the crofter has long had to look for some complementary economic activity, be it forestry or fishing, weaving or tourism. Today it could be tele-working.

It is now more important than ever to allow the modern crofter greater economic opportunity and no longer tie him or her to agriculture as a primary function. Across the European Union the whole focus is shifting from the production that created surpluses, to rural stewardship and environmental management. Against such a political backcloth we would be failing the crofting community dreadfully if we were to insist that it continue to be shackled to the old Europe and its ways. We don't want crofting to be smothered by the past.

That does not mean, however, that agricultural activity will be discouraged. Indeed niche markets for local lamb or organic produce, for example, will continue to provide the mainstay for many. I don't think that will change. But there are other opportunities which we must allow crofters to exploit.

These will change and evolve over time. At present there is enormous activity surrounding the development of the renewable energy industry and Scotland's croftlands are nearly all in geographical position to exploit either wind, wave or tidal power. It could be on the smallest scale, or something more ambitious. But we are determined that our crofters should be allowed, indeed encouraged, to benefit from such developments which have the potential to transform the economic prospects for some of our more fragile communities. It would be negligent of us not to do so.

We can't find ourselves lamenting lost opportunities when the Crofters Commission comes to celebrate its centenary. I am confident that in fifty years time our unique crofting system will have prospered, but still doing what it was set up to do – ensuring human voices are still heard in the communities carved out of a sad period in our history. •

'I am confident that in fifty years time our unique crofting system will have prospered, but still doing what it was set up to do – ensuring human voices are still heard in the communities carved out of a sad period in our history.'

Dry Stane Dyker, Burra, Shetland

Raasay wall

Cailean Maclean

Crofting People and Politics

INTRODUCTION

Shane Rankin
Chief Executive
Crofters Commission

Shane Rankin

Marking the fiftieth anniversary of a government agency is in some respects an odd thing to do. An agency surely just gets on with its administrative duties, responding to changes of government and legislation as they come along. Well yes, but it was unusual for agencies in the second half of the twentieth century to survive intact for several decades without at least a change of name or a re-orientation. Yet this is what the Crofters Commission has managed, not only survived doing largely what it was charged with doing in 1955, but still with the same name.

The name may be the clue to survival. The name harks back to the Crofters Commission of 1886 when crofting was formalised in legislation to restore order and harmony to the communities where these small agricultural holdings sustained so many people.

The Commission of the 1880s only existed for a decade or two until the government's Board of Agriculture and the Scottish Land Court took over its responsibilities. This first Commission was warmly regarded for the security and protections it brought to crofters and their communities. It is no real surprise that the Taylor Committee when it sought to revitalise crofting in the 1950s suggested a new Crofters Commission be created.

So crofting comes from a turbulent time in the history of the Highlands and Islands and one Crofters Commission or another has played a significant part in the evolution of crofting.

For some people however, crofting appears not to have evolved much in the past one hundred years or so, let alone over the past fifty years. Many crofters, and others believe crofting rights and responsibilities have not changed significantly over these years. Knowledge of crofting law has

'It was unusual for agencies in the second half of the twentieth century to survive intact for several decades without at least a change of name or a re-orientation. Yet this is what the Crofters Commission has managed, not only survived doing largely what it was charged with doing in 1955, but still with the same name.'

been handed down from generation to generation without benefiting from regular update. Yet, there has been a significant piece of crofting legislation in each decade since the 1950s. So, on the legal side of crofting, the bread and butter part for the Crofters Commission's activities, there has been major evolution over fifty years.

Of course, this legislation-inspired evolution in crofting did not just happen. It was prompted by many wider political, economic or social circumstances. It is important therefore in introducing the very human and personal articles in this book to put them in some kind of context, or at least demonstrate that there were wider events at work.

A good starting point is the terms of reference for the Commission of Enquiry into Crofting Conditions (Taylor Committee):

'to review crofting conditions with special reference to the secure establishment of a small-holding population making full use of agricultural resources and deriving maximum economic benefit'.

In 1951 this task was inevitably influenced by UK-wide postwar interest in social conditions but also by strategic concerns over maximising food production for national security in the event of further war. Only a few years previously major land use planning legislation was introduced to control for the first time the development of houses and factories in order to protect good agricultural land for food production.

The buoyant economic times of the 1960s, growing faith in science and technology impacted on the crofting areas. Agricultural science suggested that the ultimate viable croft unit could be created. It was all just a matter of critical mass, crofts should be amalgamated, land improved, government should organise demonstration crofts and provide technical advisory services. The Crofters Commission set about its role amalgamating, resisting the division of crofts and re-organising townships confident that ideal crofts and townships were achievable.

Crofting People and Politics

By the 1970s the Crofters Commission realised that science, financial support for croft development, and critical mass were not enough to revitalise crofting. Liberating crofters from the shackles of the tenancy system was the solution. Owner occupation of the small farms in Ireland and Orkney during the decades around 1900 had released enterprise and sustained rural populations. This was the big idea for crofting in the 1970s and the subsequent legislation is still discussed fiercely by those who resisted the concept then and those who have benefited from it since.

Perhaps the most significant event for crofting over the five decades happened in the 1970s. The United Kingdom joined the European Economic Community and the Common Agricultural Policy (CAP). Support for crofting agriculture ensued and supplemented the crofter-specific grants already available. Market support brought financial stability for crofters but it also encouraged their production to focus on subsidies rather than market demand. This has left them exposed in the global agricultural markets of 2005.

It is a cruel irony that in the early years of the twenty-first century the continuing expansion of the European community into the agriculture-dominated economies of Eastern Europe is bringing radical change to the CAP and crofting agriculture. Who would have thought that the concerns over national food security in the 1950s would become insignificant through ever-closer political and economic union with 26 member states across Europe?

Of course these big events encouraged change in the crofting communities, but so did more practical and personal opportunities. The growth of the North Sea oil industry created employment for crofters who could work away earning good money while returning regularly to work the croft.

Improving road, ferry and air-links in the Highlands and Islands helped make many changes possible. European regional policy provided financial

'The name may be the clue to survival. The name harks back to the Crofters Commission of 1886 when crofting was formalised in legislation to restore order and harmony to the communities where these small agricultural holdings sustained so many people.'

aid to the public bodies to make strategic investments in critical infrastructure – in roads, airports, causeways, harbours and so much else. The integrated development programmes for agriculture and economic development in the Western Isles in the 1980s were major influences on crofting in that decade. The impact of the financial aid of these programmes and that time is still visible in the fences and land improvements on crofts and townships.

Inevitably there were also local events that had huge impacts in some crofting areas and none on others. Shetland, always independent minded, struck its own deal with the oil companies in the 1970s creating a massive income stream for these islands. Through the decades that followed this income sustained public services, improved infrastructure, aided local economic development and otherwise bolstered self-confidence in that community.

But if the 1980s were a period of economic progress in the crofting counties they were also a time when politics reflected some of the wider mood of the United Kingdom. Politics became more polarised, interest groups and pressure groups came to the fore, organised opposition outside parliament became commonplace. The time was right for the re-emergence of the Crofters Union.

It was something of this 1980s political mood that carried over into the 1990s and the first community buyouts of crofting estates. Estate owners may have become more confident in free market Britain but crofting communities were not going to sit back and have their land traded around them. The crofting communities of Assynt and Borve and Annishader were at the forefront and they paved the way for land reform legislation in post-devolution Scotland.

Inevitably this introduction has passed quickly over only some of the major events that changed crofting and crofting communities. The articles that follow are personal accounts of an aspect of crofting that interests the writer. This is not history in any complete sense, but is history of the detail, the politics, the administration, the family events, the emotions and the angst. These pieces are a flavour of what it was like to live through five decades of crofting and the Crofters Commission. •

The Crofters Commission Board 1955
(left to right from top) A.R. MacKenzie, J. McNaughton,
Capt. D.A. MacLachlan, Sir Robert Urquhart (chairman), J.S. Grant,
J.A. Johnstone, D.J. MacCuish (secretary)

CROFTING
– LOOKING TO THE FUTURE

CROITEARACHD
– A'COIMHID RIS AN AM RI TEACHD

David Green
Chairman, Crofters Commission

Am fear nach seall roimhe seallaidh e 'na dheidh

The one who does not look forward will look back

David Green

Likewise crofting has to look forward and not let the shadow of the Clearances cloud over a very bright future. The six articles commissioned, generously flavoured with fondness and passion, contain all the crofting elements and emotions as they too look forward. Romanticism and nostalgia, two essential crofting components, set the scene for a twenty first century crofting vision of opportunity for land, people, and culture.

Romance introduced me to crofting in remote Wester Ross. I was hooked, after falling for a crofter's daughter and Achiltibuie at the same time. Deep down, I knew that one day I would set up home in this place of indescribable beauty to begin my life's crofting chapter.

But too much nostalgia can be unhealthy and crofting should beware lest it decays like old peats left on the bank.

Crofting must continue to prove to Holyrood, Westminster and Europe that it is delivering as a model for land use and rural development, in order to ensure ongoing support from these quarters.

Crofting has already delivered on some of the rarest environments in the world. Most of Scotland's machairs have been looked after sustainably

> **'But too much nostalgia can be unhealthy and crofting should beware lest it decays like old peats left on the bank.'**

over many generations by crofters before the concept of sustainable development was even invented.

More recently, rural stewardship schemes benefit the land. Using unharvested crops or water margins etc, they deliver the biodiversity much valued now in Scotland and Europe.

Land and people are the lifeblood of crofting. They breathe life and colour into its culture. It was indeed no accident that the cultural Feis movement began in the crofting counties. Its rapid expansion is inextricably linked to the nucleus of Gaelic culture sustained by crofting in the North and West. Moving up to Shetland how enjoyable to munch tasty 'eight o clocks' while discussing how new crofts could contribute towards development in their Initiative at the Edge areas.

The twenty first century vision will continue to be 'more sustainable crofting communities' as the Scottish Executive state in the draft Crofting Reform Bill. The Hydro Board may have put lights in the Glens but the crofters switched them on. Indeed, new crofts will have a crucial role keeping lights on, schools open and culture alive.

Click on fast forward to 2030 with the 'Creative Crofting Task Force' now based in Stornoway or Lerwick supported by Rural Development Offices throughout Scotland. Crofting regulation will be through the 'Crofters Toolkit.Com' website.

Thousands of new crofts will have been created combining organics, woodland, tourism and renewables from Fetlar to Arran. Strict entrance criteria are linked to sustaining the community. Entrants must undertake compulsory vocational training courses from the University of the Highlands and Islands available in both Gaelic and Shaetlan, taught by retiring crofters.

Kevin from Tiree, one of those croft entrants, won the European Young Entrepreneur of the Year Award for his 'Turf and Surf' business. His father secured his future on the island with the Scottish Executive's civil service relocation at the turn of the century. And now Kevin markets his father's quality beef alongside his windsurfing enterprise on his croft by the Atlantic.

Ambitious yes – but, with one fell swoop, new crofts can help put young folk back working the land with a secure home as well as a base for a business – just look at Jura now! The revitalised Croft Entrant Scheme and a targeted Absentee Initiative can help plug the 16-40 age gap missing from the Highlands and Islands population today.

Community ownership will be integral to crofting's future.

The most recent community buyout of the iconic mountains of Suilven and Canisp and 40,000 acres of Glencanisp and Drumrunie deer forests, brought another huge chunk of land back to the people. The local primary school is facing closure. New crofts already on the drawing board in Assynt awaiting the new legislation could prevent this. While in North Harris after their buy out one of the locals said, 'We still have our problems and challenges but they are now OUR problems and challenges.' Land reform has galvanised these communities to take advantage of all the opportunities ranging from housing, deer management, woodland and renewables.

Over the next fifty years the Crofters Commission, already open and accountable, must display more dynamism and leadership. It has to build on the existing meaningful partnerships which have produced eighty grass roots projects involving croft walks or community cattle schemes to achieve that vision of sustainability.

For the 30,000 people who make up our crofting families there are plenty opportunities to develop their own vision. The internet has heralded the arrival of the tele-crofter, opening a worldwide employment door hitherto kept firmly shut by the remoteness of the crofting community. There is an opportunity too for the crofter forester or the traditional crofter making local produce, to be part of the wider community's vision.

Will these people be allowed to speculate with a clear conscience in the

"Crofting gave me a real home and an enviable, carefree upbringing together with a sense of identity for my family. Even when that identity meant an aching back at the clipping, or driving rain seeping into my bones at the fank, I still enjoyed the crack. There is plenty space for others to do something similar."

coming years? Although I will not on principle buy or sell my croft, is it wrong if market forces are working for you to realise a lifetime's investment? The land, your pension, or your children's future may depend upon this.

Renewables and housing will be part of crofting's future. Some 10% of Scotland is under crofting tenure often beside the coast. Crofting communities have real potential to benefit from renewables or play their part in the provision of housing on common grazings near settlements and create new croft land nearby.

Increasingly in the future a lot of people will want to live in a crofting community. Therefore, care must be taken by planners, developers and crofters not to spoil that sense of place and space that epitomises that community. If the bull park, or the rock where the botachs used to gather and blether has a local community value, planners need to be engaged to ensure they stay protected in the local plan.

Crofting gave me a real home and an enviable, carefree upbringing together with a sense of identity for my family. Even when that identity meant an aching back at the clipping, or driving rain seeping into my bones at the fank, I still enjoyed the crack. There is plenty space for others to do something similar.

With care, commitment and creativity crofting can make a positive contribution to rural development into the future. It has an incredible history. It will have a fantastic future, with the help of the old to guide and inspire and maybe let go, while the young enthuse and commit, filling the schools and the glens.

As they say in Shaetlan:
'Him at winna when he may, sanna when he wid.'

Take opportunities when they come or they may not return.

John Macdonald
weaving in 1960

Tending the beasts

23

Staffin, Skye

Crofting People and Politics

Cailean Maclean

Tarskavaig, Sleat, Isle of Skye

'We are well aware that the problem of the crofting counties cannot be stated solely in terms of economic or amenities or food production. A way of life is involved and deep-rooted feelings for the traditional life of the community, and for the land which ancestral toil has won from the wild.'

Report of the Commission of Enquiry into Crofting Condition April 1954

'We have begun our work with a due sense of its urgency and importance, holding it to be a true proposition that the Highlands of Scotland have long been undervalued. We see ourselves as the latest recruits for the campaign, steadily if slowly unfolding over recent years, to revive the Highlands.'

First Annual Report of the Crofters Commission December 1956

Crofting at Tingwall, Shetland

1. NOT BORN EVERY MINUTE

Crofting 1950s
Drew Ratter

Drew Ratter was born in Ollaberry in Shetland, where his family have been crofters as far back as anybody can tell. He grew up there, and in his younger days studied at the Universities of Sussex, Massachusetts and Edinburgh, before marrying and sellling back on the family croft. During 20 years of self employment as a crofter, he has written and spoken extensively on crofting and its future, and is currently a board member of HIE as well as of the Crofters Commission, and sits on Shetland Islands Council where he is Chairman of Economic Development.

I KNOW that the 1950s is the first decade in which I can say: 'I mind'. So, that, to a fair extent, is what I am going to do. I am going to cast among what I can mind, and hence try to put a finger or two upon crofting in the 1950s, the ten years of the life of the Crofter's Commission given to me to ponder. Well five, anyway, as it was only born in 1955, when I was three, and mind very little.

I mind, and the more I think about it the fresher and closer it comes to me. I had started out my research with more of an idea of a journey through historical documents. While on that course, I certainly found some interesting fragments, such as that the first Chairman of the Crofter's Commission was Sir Robert Urquhart, who was particularly to be recommended on account of his time in the Levant Consular Service.

I offer that without comment, apart from the fact that he and his two Gaelic-speaking followers at the time were extremely well paid. £3000 and £2000 per annum, part time, in the mid 1950s. A roadman, such as my father, at that period would have been doing well to make £5 a week.

I also came across a very lively account in the Shetland Times in July of 1955, of Mr N.O.M. Cameron, proprietor of the Garth Estate, and his application to the Land Court to increase his rents. Clearly a witty man, his case seemed to be that he was stuck with this crofting land, could not, as royalty might, abdicate, and that purchasers for crofting estates: 'were not born every minute. The actual frequency was about two in a century!'

At the same time, while being arrested by such pithy articles, I was grieved to find, in 1953, 1954, and 1955, no interest whatsoever expressed by the Shetland Times (as it remains today, a genuine focus for lively local debate) in the Taylor Commission and its outcomes. There was

> '**In fact, in the late 1950s, I can mind as well the last wave of ten pound emigration from around our part of Shetland to New Zealand and bairns leaving the Ollaberry school to go. I have no doubt that without the essential buffer of the croft, more would have followed.**'

a bald report of the commission being set up, another couple on how the council intended to respond, and how after a bit, meetings in Shetland had been set up. But none of the lively public debate I had expected, and none of the urgency you get reading the proceedings of the Napier Commission, some seventy years earlier, and reported verbatim by both of Shetland's newspapers. It was in light of this that my original plan had to be amended.

Instead, still going by the Times, all the way though those particular three years, crofting was obviously important in Shetland, and had a solid presence in the letters page, with exactly the same sort of concerns which are expressed today. Stock prices, the next big thing (deep litter hens), the inability of young crofters to get crofts, a future for Shetland wool and hosiery. Future plans for exporting chilled lamb. Interestingly, and I suppose irrelevantly here, I also found a proposal for three to four megawatt wind farms on Shetland hill tops, and what might just as well have been a contemporary analysis of why these would be a benefit. In 1952!

So that would be the background to any crofting activity in the Shetland of the 1950s. A lively debate, certainly, but the Taylor Commission does not seem to have formed a major part of it.

As to crofting itself in the 1950s. What part did it play? Well, the Shetland economy has been a series of short booms and long busts over a very long period. World War II was a boom economically, in a way World War I was not. There was a lot of construction activity here, there were markets for gansies, there were all sorts of things going on, which all ceased quite abruptly in 1945. And we never had the postwar boom which transformed much of the UK.

In fact, in the late 1950s, I can mind as well the last wave of ten pound emigration from around our part of Shetland, to New Zealand, and bairns leaving the Ollaberry school to go. I have no doubt that, without the essential buffer of the croft, more would have followed.

Shaetlan words

Gansies: woollen jersies

Hence, a family in Shetland, on a croft, spent the 1950s pretty preoccupied with finding work. There would have been more or less no paid outside work for women, with the expansion of knitwear really only coming to pass in the 1960s. Very little for men either, in rural Shetland. Which likewise was nothing new.

Roadmen, working for da coonty, often only had summer work and most were paid off in winter. My father was one of these, starting the 1950s as a lobster fisherman and jobbing builder, moving to work in a short-lived and abjectly badly run iron ore mine in Sullom, and then moving on, through Callanders, to council roads and quarry work, where he managed to stay on summer and winter for the next decade. Then he made the decision, he among many others at the end of the 1960s, to try to be a full-time crofter. This last he stuck to till he retired towards the end of the 1980s, fencing and reseeding on a considerable scale, and pursuing the economically viable unit.

For the Crofters Commission, and the College, and the Department, there was a sort of 1960s convention that that was 12 cows and 100 ewes. It certainly proved a kind of mirage, that 'economic unit'. Always sort of on the horizon, with glimpses caught only out of the corner of the eye; never by looking direct. We have stopped looking for it now, but only very recently, in Shetland at least.

The role of crofting for us in the 1950s? Well, we had no croft at that time, with succession passing our current land to us in the mid 1960s. However, both sides of the family were crofters, and all in the neighbourhood, so we benefited from that, and were constantly engaged with it.

I mind again. I mind very clearly all the time I spent with my grandmother and separately my grand aunt, going around the hill in voar time, studying for our own sheep with binoculars and a knowledge of where they would be, catching lambs and caddling them with our own colour of paint, querving hay, carrying it in in a maishie, bigging desses. Setting plant, hoeing, scraping and heaping, working in the peats.

'I mind one of the things us bairns would occasionally discuss was what houses in the neighbourhood we would have to knock on the door before we went in. There were very few; the community was very egalitarian, and to knock on a neighbour's door would have been queer; almost an insult.'

Da county: the council

Caddling: applying identifying paint marks

Querving: turning swathes with a rake to aid curing

Maishie: an affair of rope and net for carrying hay

Bigging: building

Desses: large haystacks for winter storage

Putting the kye to the hill. The great days of apportionments and reseeding had not got going really at all, and did not come to much hereabouts, apart from a few pioneering spirits, till the late sixties. Hence the bairns were often sent out in the morning to put the kye to the hill, out on to the scattald, and to fetch them at night, with a dockan in hand as a switch to urge them on.

Every decent day had a whole set of necessary tasks awaiting it, and leisure and pleasure might be a night at the eela, annowing around the right places, catching mackerel, or more commonly, piltocks. I mind one year when I was quite young that my grandfather took a serious notion in the wylk ebb, gathering what I think sooth folk call winkles, for sale to save enough money for Christmas. I spent a lot of time with him in the bottom of the ebb when the new moon came, what we call da strem.

I have a clear minding of much of that kind of activity, and a community which probably more belongs to the nineteenth even, than the twentieth century. Still a great lot of going among the neighbours' houses about the night, and a kind of strong communal feeling. I mind one of the things us bairns would occasionally discuss was what houses in the neighbourhood we would have to knock on the door before we went in.

There were very few; the community was very egalitarian, and to knock on a neighbour's door would have been queer; almost an insult. I can not analyse with concrete evidence, but I do think that those Shetland crofters I mind as a bairn were the last of the Victorians. They were, for example, a lot of the people I had most to do with, women who had perhaps had prospects of marrying before World War I, and had to make a different sort of life afterwards.

Those Shetland Victorians, I think, had a consciousness formed by Christianity, but it appears to me a form of Christianity which was not endlessly judgemental and censorious, but which said folk should be good to each other. I am not trying to hark back to a golden age here, because I

Bairns: children

Kye: cattle

Scattald: common grazing

Dockan: common dock

Eela: The crofter's inshore line fishing, for young saithe mostly

Annowing: rowing slowly

Piltocks: saithe up to two years old

Wylks: winkles

Sooth folk: everybody but Shetlanders

Ebb: from high to low watermark

Da Strem: the maximum tides coinciding with the new moon

Crofting People and Politics

think that moment was relatively brief. The 1830s and 1840s in Shetland were certainly a nightmare of famine and want.

I wonder though, if it is too fanciful to bookend a pretty attractive period in Shetland between the first Crofting Act, and the opening up of the new materialism, 1960s-70s, and getting worse? It would not be a bad comment to be able to make about crofting. Note that by that new materialism, the reference is not Shetland, though it is of course as much core to existence there as elsewhere, but to the phase of capitalism we are currently resident within, where consumption by the many is more central to keeping things going than it has ever been. In Shetland still, I think anyway, much that was positive has been retained from those days. Certainly that spirit of egalitarianism is still strong.

I mind also electrification, the hydro, that other great anchor of highland and island population. My father and my uncle and most of the men of the neighbourhood went to work for Callenders Cables, putting in the new Shetland grid. I mind reading (I was an avid and early reader, and of John Bunyan, R.M. Ballantyne, and Zane Grey) by the light of the tilley lamp, and after bed time, the oil lamp. Maybe that is what gave me such bad eyesight? Anyway, it came to an end in 1959 when the house was wired, and shortly came another thing which changed lives and diets on the croft, the deep freeze. We still like saat fish and reestit mutton, but now we eat them because we relish them, not daily all winter.

The 1950s were days when the great Shetland sheep economy was still, if not an infant, far from fully grown. I went to the Ronas hill sheep, to Fjeal, with my granny, and there were fewer excellent trials dogs, much more flapping of pinnies, and much more laborious ways of doing things. For instance, Ronas hill being far too big to wander over caddling lambs, so the system there in those days meant painting different combinations of marks on all the lambs, putting them and all the ewes in an outer pen, then watching out and noting which lamb paired up with which ewe.

Reestit mutton: mutton salted and dried over a peat fire

That sheep economy, of course, nurtured by Sheep Annual Premium, grew into a veritable giant in the 1990s. It is now, deprived of that rich nutrition, shrinking back, and it will be interesting to see how the hills develop from now, with such stress being put on environmental outcomes, and public goods.

But just now, on the 1950s, if you draw anything from what I mind, I hope it is that crofting was very, very, important to pretty well all of the folk of rural Shetland. The need for milk and a milking cow was absolute and immediate, without peats, and with no money to buy other fuel, the winters would have been long and cold – incidentally, I also mind a series of exceptionally snowy winters!

Tatties and reestit mutton, saat fish, saat herring, were still very much the winter staple. And a croft house, which had no rent to be paid on it, and the ownership of which was entirely unchallenged. These featured high in a world where employment and the next pay packet was very insecure. Such was its place in the unspoken assumptions of daily life in rural Shetland.

Its place in the public consciousness of Shetland folk was likewise prominent. A firm consensus existed then, as now, that Shetland's main resources were either on the land, or in the sea. There was a close interest in the Flock Book sales, just as today, with the Shetland Times printing a sales report with prices, just as today.

There was, in 1954, in February, started a serious debate on using the plant of the Herring Industry Board so that lambs in Shetland could be slaughtered, then chilled and shipped. This, it was suggested could be 'the salvation of Shetland'. It was pointed out that before the war, great numbers of lambs went south as store lambs and 'it would be a disaster for Shetland if that happened again, as it was a proper gamble.' Whether it was a disaster or not, the latter is what happened.

At the Althing, in Tingwall, in February two years before, an exceptionally well argued debate between Prophet Smith and John Jamieson, with Mortimer Manson and Charles Arthur seconding took on the motion 'Shetland does not regret the Crofters' Act'. This is very fully reported, and certainly demonstrates that a high degree of the arcane on such a subject could draw a wide audience. Just as it can today.

The 1950s, then. A time when crofting was on the cusp of change, a time when much development, albeit in the spirit of food security, was just beginning, for crofters and crofters. The 1950s Crofters Commission was very much part of that, and the vision developed then and carried forward, had quite a bit of mileage and oomph in it. I wonder if this is another such time? I wonder, today, if the new revamped Crofters Commission will demonstrate that kind of vision and leadership and work with crofters to create and realise a renewed positive vision?

There is a new one available, there are tremendous possibilities, say in the creation of crofts, and in crofting as a tool for rural regeneration. As far as I can see, the Crofters Commission is in the best position to pick up that vision and inspire others with it, if its members choose to.   •

Caílean Maclean

Crofting at Uig, Skye

Crofting People and Politics

2. WALKING AND CROFTING

The 1960s
Angus Macdonald

Angus Macdonald was born on the Island of Lewis. A native Gaelic speaker, he graduated from the University of Glasgow with a degree in English Literature and Political Economy. He worked the family croft while employed at Lewis Offshore's Arnish yard and during a short spell teaching at the Nicolson Institute where he had himself received his secondary education. He joined the BBC's Gaelic radio service in 1983, before becoming Senior Producer at BBC Highland in 1987. He has been a freelance journalist and broadcaster since 1993, and lives with his wife Alison and three children, John, Kirsten and Calum in Inverness.

The Second World War which had ended less than twenty years before, helped shape the community of Swordale – men and women who had borne the heat of battle, the threat of death and the privation of a war that threatened civilisation. Some had shouldered great responsibilities, had emerged as leaders and had chosen to return. Some had furthered their education and were now teachers, doctors or nurses. Most had returned to eke a living out of fishing, weaving, working for the County and wrestling a few acres hard won from peat bog and cliff top by themselves or their ancestors.

For many, school had finished at 14 years of age, but the depth of their analysis of local, national and world events, founded on the moral certitude of an unwavering faith, would have outshone university professors.

We started the croft work when we started walking. Gathering eggs or potatoes, feeding pet lambs and the sheep, gathering peats on the moor, or taking bottles of milk to elderly neighbours when the cow had calved. As we grew, we learned the spade, the tairsgeir, the grap (a fork was for hay or for holding in your left hand at the table), the hammer and the shears. The scythe was overtaken by the tractor mower before the skill could be honed to anything remotely like the poetry in motion that was my father, cutting grass or oats into long, regular swathes in the buzzing warmth of the hot summers and fruitful autumns. And slowly, the land, the sea, the people and the work insinuated itself into the blood, leaving for the exile a restlessness of spirit that nothing else of this world can satisfy.

'Between 1948 and September 1964 no fewer than 985 new croft houses have been built and 2,011 croft houses substantially improved.' [1]

My memory of JF Kennedy's assassination is vague. I cannot remember where I was, probably in bed, although I can remember adults worried for the future of the world, when they thought we were out of earshot. I remember Robert Kennedy's assassination five years later, horrified that a famous man could be shot, and listening intently, with the lights out, to the old radio in our kitchen, which glowed yellow and green.

Another event in 1963 had a far greater impact – my brother was born. Like the rest of us, he was born in the house built by my father fifteen years earlier. The house had featured in the Daily Record in 1948 as the first hipped-roof bungalow to be built by a crofter in Lewis after the war. While my two older sisters and I checked the lambing, the fearsome nurse from Ness and the doctor, who was dressed in orange brace-and-bib oilskin trousers, got busy. Later my mother lay proudly beside a little figure, still looking slightly damp, but with the great potential of playing football in a few years' time.

The coming of TV in the mid-60s accelerated change in the village. At first, with TV in just three houses, they became the new tighean-ceilidh. Big events, such as the World Cup Final in 1966, or Neil Armstrong landing on the moon on my grandfather's birthday in 1969, drew us round and conversation flowed around the programmes and tea, scones and oatcakes. Later, TVs fragmented the community, and people were unwilling to visit neighbours in the evenings after work was done.

We laughed then at mailboat stoppages. Our link with the mainland was the 'Loch Seaforth', which sailed in weather that would make present day passengers reach for the writs. We could have outlasted a siege, missing perhaps sugar, salt and flour, but never lacking meat or fish – mainly herring. Potatoes and vegetables lasted nearly all year, if you got the sloc right and 'earlies' planted in time. Now of course everything is more modern. We buy organic produce off the supermarket shelf and two days of rough weather causes blind panic in island supermarkets.

Getting into Stornoway, five miles away, where the Board store and the

Gaelic words

tairsgeir: peat-cutter

grap: graipe

sloc: earth storage pit

Board office were to be found was a rare treat, a bus ride, with Woolies full of unattainable wonder. Very few in the village could afford cars, because money was tight. There was a bright side. My uncle Norman, who lived across the road, had no children of his own. He worked for the building contractor Hughsons in Stornoway as well as working the croft. Every Friday he brought home in the haversack, which had held his gasmask during the War, crisps he had picked up when having his pint in the Neptune, or liquorice pipes, penny toffees or hard-boiled fruit-flavoured sweets bought in Cabrelli's on his way to the bus.

We sold the cattle in the late 60s. By then the 'Frying Pan's' daily milk delivery and the availability of other dairy products from the vans and the Post Office (Tigh 'an Sheumais, the local debating chamber and nerve-centre of news and gossip) had made the cow redundant and rearing calves no longer cost-effective. With them went the daily mucking out, the fight with the biota to make the butter form, and the morning walk to the rough pasture behind the village. One of my earliest memories is competing with Domhnull Chailein, who seemed as old as a Druid, which of us could walk deeper into Loch Drolabhat on one of these mornings. Even without the cattle, there was still plenty of manure available in the spring when the oisgean, which had been over-wintered in the shed behind the byre, were released. Tractor-loads of seaweed completed the fertilising mix.

The sea too provided shingle for paths and pebble dash, or for the poured concrete in the walls of our house. It yielded razorfish at Easter, saithe, pollack, wrasse, codling and edible crabs in the summer, and cuddies caught in a poca-chudaig taken home by the pailful as the dark evenings of autumn crept in. The older people swore by the sabhs as a cure-all.

'The essential requirement is to ensure that there are employments and occupations for the occupants of the crofts and their families. This need has been fortunately met to some extent on Lewis by the Harris Tweed industry, while employment in the Merchant Navy has usefully

---

tighean-ceilidh: ceilidh houses
biota: butter churn
oisgean: yearling lambs
poca-chudaig: cuddy bag-net
sabhs: fish soup

'**Transcending the crofting system that made it possible, and the Gaelic that gave them voice in work, play, song and worship, the people rise in memory like heroes of old striding across the horizon. . .'**

supplemented the employment available on the crofts and in the Harris Tweed industry.'[2]

My father, who had been a fisherman and then in the Navy before first building our own house, and then a number of others, changed from builder to Harris Tweed weaver with the mid-60s unprecedented boom in tweed sales. The Hattersley loom was like an over-sensitive lover. One touch too tight, and the mood was off. Sometimes the loom went so far awry, the shuttles flew like Exocets, leaving the V-lined partition wall in the byre, pock-marked like a Beirut 1970s high-rise.

Two loom doctors were always on hand, Alasdair a' Chaiptein, who also did an interesting line in herbal remedies and back of the lorry materials, and Pords, another war veteran, a romantic, a breeder of sheep and walker of moors, and a man of God. In the twilight zone of the Tweed industry, my father got to know Eddie Gray, who managed to steer tweeds in his direction, even when the distribution system in Stornoway tried to play favourites with boys from the town. One persistent batch of clerical grey twill weave, which seemed to be in endless demand, was destined to be turned into burial suits for rich Americans, according to the mill grapevine.

Controversy came in many guises. The village was split following a row in the church in the early 60s, which eventually caused two Free Church congregations to be formed in the Point area – as the Preacher said centuries before, there was nothing new under the sun. Trouble flared too over that other source of international bloodshed – land. Sly and not-so-sly boundary changes occurred, when new fences were being built to enclose what had once been open adjacent crofts, or when old fences were being replaced. The range wars over peats erupted regularly, when the seven tairsgeir length separation between peat banks was not rigorously observed. Rows broke out over which end of the village was due to have their peat road repaired using gravel from the rich-orange fine-gravel pit shared by the two villages of Knock and Swordale. The longest

Crofting People and Politics

lasting vendettas were over disputed land inheritance rights. One family experienced several newborn deaths. The problem could probably have been cured now, but then people said this was a breitheanas for a croft obtained fraudulently in the past.

'They drew their strength from the land on which they stood and from the Rock on which their feet had been placed.'

> 'If one had to look for a way of life which could keep that number of people in such relative intractable territory, it would be difficult to contrive a better system.' (First report of the HIDB)

As the years passed, Government help for crofting agriculture improved. My father came back from evening meetings with new ideas on sheep breeding and Board rams. New grass mixes and feed concentrates would ensure better sheep milk yields at lambing. Filling in 'the returns' yielded better returns itself. The village invested in a 'prairie' – a reseeding scheme behind the village which, together with the grazing on the Barvas Moor, would help carry larger numbers of sheep through the year, while relieving pressure on the crofts, and leaving more inbye area for cropping. The sand left over from de-acidifying the 'prairie's' peaty soil, became the haunt of rabbits, under-employed collies with mining instincts and occasionally, village children, before being reclaimed by the heather. Drainage and fencing schemes, and later sheds and byres also appeared with grant and loan packages and gradually the old tobhtaichean, including the last inhabited blackhouse in the village, disappeared to be replaced by new and improved houses strung along both sides of the village road.

Transcending the crofting system that made it possible, and the Gaelic that gave them voice in work, play, song and worship, the people rise in memory like heroes of old striding across the horizon. My two auntie Marys who had been herring gutters – hard, unrelenting, financially unrewarding work, a fish-scale's thickness from slavery – had participated in an unsuccessful strike in Yarmouth in the 1930s to raise pay rates. Rod, a sailor in the Merchant Navy, had been awarded the DSM for heroic action in the War. My uncle Norman, whose stories were themselves legendary,

breitheanas: a judgement

tobhtaichean: thatched house walls

had survived an attempt on his life during a wartime spying mission in Norway. Tojan had helped build Dounreay. Domhnull Iain could knock a seagull out of the sky with a stone, Aonghas Alasdair had telescopic eyesight, Cully Beag, after years in the Falklands could shear with both hands, Tenant could speak like a poet and Calum Dhomnuill and Tarmod Beag could climb any cliff bordering the sea. My mother, Anna Bheag, always quiet, had been a wartime lumberjill, and my father, Iain Eachainn, always balaisteach, would have laughed at the phrase 'career-change', had it been in his lexicon.

How to encompass the richness of growing into adulthood surrounded by men and women of such stature? How to measure the depth of their lives beside which the business, entertainment, financial, industrial, intellectual and political elite appear as transient, inconsequential, effete and without hinterland? They drew their strength from the land on which they stood and from the Rock on which their feet had been placed.

I was born too late to appreciate the 1960s. The power of flowers, and their various extracts, passed me by and the swooning of my older sisters over the Beatles, Elvis and Cliff Richard seemed an aberration. My defining moments were more mundane, and involved characters who never strode the world stage – although they could have done. As the 1960s closed, secondary education in the Nicolson Institute beckoned and beyond that the open door to the wider world.

Postscript and future

My grandfather was born in 1886, the year of the first Crofters Act. The Crofters Commission's fiftieth anniversary coincides with legislation, of equally fundamental importance. Crofting, a protected agricultural tenure, will be exposed to market forces and without protection the beauty of crofting communities, houses surrounded by their own land, will change. Lights in the glen are intrinsically more valuable than glens supporting nothing but the whim of the sporting rich. Croft land must not be smothered in the dense housing and industrial development that changed

balaisteach: steady, balanced

places such as Inverness from a unique town to a city of chain store, franchise, rat-cage anonymity. Crofting can bring new communities into existence and should be extended throughout the millions of barren hectares in the Highlands and Islands. Crofting agriculture will die unless legislators make the small-scale organic farming, inherent in the crofting system, pay in remote areas. Instead of urbanising hard-won croft land, further alienating people from their natural ties with the land, planners, environmentalists and legislators should 'croftise' all new urban developments. The old warning still stands: 'Woe unto them that join house to house, that lay field to field, till there be no place, that they may be placed alone in the midst of the earth!' (Isaiah 5:8) •

Notes

(1) 'Land Use in the Highlands and Islands' p20 – Advisory Panel on the Highlands and Islands, report to the Secretary of State for Scotland 27th October 1964.

(2) Ibid p14

Laying creels, Eriskay

Crofting and fishing at Elgol. Isle of Skye

Cailean Maclean

Crofting People and Politics

3. TENURE AND THE MARKET

The 1970s
Brian Wilson

Brian Wilson stood down at the last election after 18 years as MP for Cunninghame North. Following Labour's election to Government in 1997, he held five ministerial posts – each of which gave him an involvement in energy issues. He was the Scottish industry minister in 1997-98 and the UK energy minister from 2001-2003. When he announced his intention to leave Parliament, the Prime Minister asked him to act as his Special Representative on Overseas Trade, with a particular focus on energy issues, a role he continues to fulfill. He is now involved also in advising several energy companies – particularly in the renewables sector – and, just for a bit of light relief, has recently been appointed as a non-executive director of Celtic football club.

The major crofting issue throughout the 1970s centred on the question of owner-occupation. This was a hangover from the previous decade when the top-down movement to turn crofters into owner-occupiers had created deep divisions within crofting politics.

Because the Crofters Commission had been the principal advocate of owner-occupancy, it was not seen as a neutral upholder of the crofting interest. Indeed, the Crofters Commission was at the centre of the controversy and was far more active than any politician in advocating this fundamental change in the status of crofters.

In 1975, Margaret MacPherson – the Skye crofter who had been a member of the Taylor Committee twenty years earlier – looked back on the intervening period. She recalled that the name for the new, regulatory body which had emerged in the 1950s was chosen because the first Crofters Commission 'after the 1886 Act did such good work' in controlling croft rents and the resumption of land by the landlords.

Mrs MacPherson went on to contrast that record with the performance of the re-born Crofters Commission and in particular how it had backed off, in its early days, from the reorganisation of crofting estates. This was after the Treasury had objected to the costs involved in the proposed reorganisation of Waternish Estate – the first case study which the infant Commission had embarked upon.

'There was no point in creating a Commission to reorganise decaying townships,' wrote Margaret MacPherson, 'if they were going to fall down at the first hurdle. A determined stand can do a lot. . .' By the 1970s, the Crofters Commission had certainly abandoned any vision of reorganising the crofting townships on an area-by-area basis. Instead, it had become the prime advocate of an approach which centred largely on the rights of the individual crofter.

Margaret MacPherson summed up this position in terms which supporters of owner-occupation – notably the Crofters Commission chairman, James Shaw Grant – doubtless regarded as both political and pejorative. 'Worse was to follow,' she wrote. 'In 1968, they (the Commission) came out with proposals to do away with the Crofting Laws'. What Margaret MacPherson was referring to was the landmark document produced by the Commission under the title 'Recommendations for the Modernisation of Crofting'.

Modernisation – or abolition? That is really the debate that has gone on, in one form or another, down to the present day and while it peaked in the 1970s, it has been around – as Margaret MacPherson pointed out – since the very beginning. She wrote: 'The Taylor Commission considered the question of ownership and came down against it because private ownership of inbye land and common ownership of the grazings would not work, an argument which is as valid today as it was then.'

She continued: 'Now the Crofters Commission, set up twenty years ago to breathe life into crofting, has handed an axe to the Secretary of State to sever those laws which from 1886 onwards alone have prevented crofters from being scattered to the ends of the earth. The first Crofters Commission has been remembered all these years with affection. This Crofters Commission has not been so.'

Margaret MacPherson's writings from thirty years ago are worth quoting and considering because they represent not only the essential argument against owner-occupation but also confirm the long pedigree of this debate. The 1976 Crofting Reform Act can, within that context, be seen as a kind of half-time score rather than either the beginning or end of an argument though it is certainly true that the political debate about crofting during the 1970s carried a passion and articulacy that have subsequently been in shorter supply.

'Recommendations for the Modernisation of Crofting' promoted the idea that owner-occupancy would be cheap, easy and would not affect the status of crofters in relation to grants and other benefits. The down-payment of a sum equivalent to one year's rent, according to Shaw Grant and the Crofters Commission secretary Donald MacCuish, would be enough to convert crofting tenants into owner-occupiers. They would then be free to sell as they pleased while retaining the benefits of crofting status.

Support for this formula emanated primarily from the Isle of Lewis for reasons that remain puzzling. It is probably true that anti-landlord sentiment in Lewis was stronger than in any part of the Crofting Counties and the principle of crofters being in thrall to no landlord carried a strong rhetorical appeal. Against that was the fact that Lewis contained by far the biggest community-owned estate in the Crofting Counties – Stornoway Trust – while most of the other crofting estates were, in terms of enforcing landlords' powers, essentially moribund. In contrast, tenants enjoyed security of tenure with little external interference.

For whatever reason, owner-occupation had become the cause célèbre of the Federation of Crofters Unions – run largely from Lewis – and of the crofter-schoolmasters who dominated both Labour and crofting politics on the islands. One of these, John Murdo MacMillan, was a member of the Crofters Commission and a close ally of James Shaw Grant. The rift with those who disagreed had become bitter and was at the root of divisions within the Western Isles Labour Party which contributed to the defeat of Malcolm K. MacMillan – a resolute opponent of owner-occupation – in the 1970 General Election.

Nationally, the Tories were returned to power in that election and it soon became apparent that there was a chasm separating the tempting carrots contained in 'Recommendations for the Modernisation of Crofting' from the reality of proposed legislation. Critically, there was to be no 'big bang' approach to owner-occupation, in direct contradiction to the Crofters Commission's strongest recommendation. And, of course – coming from a Tory government – the position of crofting landlords was to be maintained

'I therefore recommend that; the Secretary of State for Scotland should, at a given date, acquire all the crofting land in the seven crofting counties. Landlords should be compensated on whatever terms are considered equitable.'

Note of Dissent
by Mrs Margaret H. MacPherson.
Member of the Commission of
Enquiry into Crofting Conditions,
April 1954

with development value of croft land, whether owner-occupied or not, retained firmly in their hands.

Even though it was brushed aside in this way, 'Recommendations for the Modernisation of Crofting' remains a seminal document for one principal reason. This is contained in its declaration: 'The Commission came to the conclusion that the only realistic choice was between conversion to owner-occupancy of all crofts on an appointed day or the retention of existing tenure'. In this respect, if in no other, Shaw Grant and MacCuish were entirely in line with the thinking of Margaret MacPherson and, indeed, the conclusion of the Taylor Commission. There could be no mixed bag of tenure and owner-occupation.

This has remained the principal fault-line in all subsequent debates about crofting reform – the incompatibility between a system of tenure, involving rights of succession and collective responsibilities, and the expectations which are created by anointing individuals with the status of property owners. Whatever the relative merits of the two concepts, the Crofters Commission was surely right to conclude that they could not co-exist within crofting townships. Yet that is precisely the circle that every subsequent attempt at crofting legislation has tried to square.

Not that the Crofters Commission held to its own philosophical position for very long once it saw the way the political wind was blowing. The idea of legislating for a wholesale, compulsory transition to owner-occupancy on a given date never seems to have been taken seriously either by the Tory government which came to power in 1970 or its Labour successors in 1974. Soon James Shaw Grant was arguing, just as enthusiastically, for the somewhat different concept of 'freedom of choice' as the basis of a gradual transition towards owner-occupation.

The Tories introduced a Bill but never got round to taking it through its Parliamentary stages, much to the irritation of the Crofters Commission leadership who quickly turned their attentions to the incoming Labour administration. Here, they enjoyed more success – though not before there was a passionate and deeply divisive argument within Labour's ranks. While William Ross, returning as Secretary of State for Scotland, almost immediately undertook to proceed with owner-occupancy legislation – albeit on more favourable terms to crofters – the Scottish Labour Party repeatedly rejected this position.

A working-party set up by Labour's Scottish Executive came up with a radically different set of proposals, under the title of the Crofter's Charter. The significance of this document – other than the historic curiosity that it represented a Labour Party policy on crofting which was rejected by a Labour Government – lies in the fact that it laid the ground for reforms which took place more than twenty years later when Labour was again in power and radical land reform was higher on its agenda. The 'crofting community right to buy' was a direct descendant of the Crofter's Charter, though still not so radical.

The Crofter's Charter called for all crofting land to be brought under the ownership of a Crofters Trust, with compensation to the landowners set at 6.3 times the annual rental income – in other words, not very much. Trustees would be elected, the Crofters Commission was to be subsumed into the Highlands and Islands Development Board and resumption values would be shared between individual crofters and the Crofters Trust. In other words, private crofting landlords were to be abolished – and the alternative was not to be state ownership but a representative, accountable body elected by crofters themselves.

The Scottish Labour Conference in March 1975 adopted the Crofter's Charter and overwhelmingly rejected the plans for owner-occupation. Subsequently, in June of that year, a specially-convened Highlands and Islands conference of the Labour Party reached the same conclusion. This gathering, in Inverness, was significant for the emergence of a new voice from Lewis. While Charles MacLeod, one of the crofter-headmasters, denounced the 'doctrinaire socialism' of the Crofter's Charter, the former Provost of Stornoway, Sandy Matheson, found 'a good deal of sense' in it and criticised only the proposed creation of another central body to administer crofting affairs. Far better, he argued, to have localised control

'This has remained the principal fault line in all subsequent debates about crofting reform – the incompatibility between a system of tenure, involving rights of succession and collective responsibilities, and the expectations which are created by anointing individuals with the status of property owners. Whatever the relative merits of the two concepts, the Crofters Commission was surely right to conclude that they could not co-exist within crofting townships. Yet that is precisely the circle that every subsequent attempt at crofting legislation has tried to square.'

modelled on the Stornoway Trust. Matheson's argument, which was well-received by the Charter's supporters, took the model one step closer to the future role of community buy-outs.

Notwithstanding such diversions, Willie Ross adhered to his owner-occupancy legislation and so, in 1976, the right of individual crofters to buy their inbye land was enshrined in law. There was a significant uptake in Caithness and some other areas where the status of crofting tenants had come to be resented rather than valued; and particularly where there were obvious possibilities for developing the land for purposes other than those associated with crofting. In the crofting heartlands, however, the uptake was very limited – not least because the message soon got through that owner-occupation would be accompanied by the phasing out and means-testing of crofting grants and loans; in direct contradiction to repeated assurances given by the Crofters Commission.

This reality was highlighted by a spectacular episode on Skye which was brought about by the arrival on the scene of a Dutch cattle-dealer and land speculator, Johannes Hellinga, who acquired the mainly crofting estate of Waternish. Hellinga quickly realised that this unfamiliar form of tenure offered him little in the form of income and significant nuisance value in the form of responsibilities. He therefore proclaimed himself a philanthropist and offered to 'sell' crofting tenants their land for five pence an acre. Most of the Scottish media swallowed Hellinga's 'generosity' hook, line and sinker. So too, unfortunately, did some of his Waternish tenants – who promptly found themselves disqualified from the familiar benefits of crofting tenure. The message reverberated rapidly round the Crofting Counties.

By the end of the decade, James Shaw Grant's successor in 1978 as chairman of the Crofters Commission, the Inverness lawyer Jeff MacLeod, was recognising that the purchase of crofts had 'ground to a halt'. Indeed, he went further and warned that the vast majority of crofters who had remained as tenants would be 'ill-advised' to buy their holdings. It was impossible by this point to avoid the conclusion that a huge amount of time and energy had been wasted on arguing over a concept that was of very little interest to most crofters or, indeed, of any value whatsoever to crofting.

However, the whole episode did give rise to one blatant deficiency – the absence of a representative voice for crofters to offset the role of the Crofters Commission which existed as the regulator of crofting but was increasingly accepted by Government as 'the voice of crofting'. There was a conflict between these two roles which had become inescapable because of the advocacy role that the commission had played during the owner-occupancy debate. By the end of the decade, this had paved the way for the arguments which would in turn lead to the formation of the Scottish Crofters Union.

The relatively esoteric debate about the status of crofters took place against a background of more generalised interest in the land question within Scotland. The advent of the North Sea oil industry – and the speculation that it inevitably gave rise to – drew attention to the fact that so much of the Highlands and Islands was owned by so few people. The legislation promoted by Shetland Isles Islands Council to bring lasting benefit to the population as a whole highlighted the fact that alternative models could and should exist. While the rights of crofting landlords were severely constrained by the Crofting Acts, mineral and sporting rights continued to reside with them – the latter, a constant source of irritation in many areas and the former a significant source of revenue.

By the late 1970s, the Highlands and Islands Development Board had drawn up plans which would have supported a community right to take over the land on which it lived. However, the moment had passed and the return to power of the Conservatives in 1979 killed off any prospect of such an initiative for the next eighteen years. In truth, however, it was not the HIDB – an economic development body rather than a political policy-maker – which should have been bringing forward such politically contentious proposals but the Government itself, as represented by the Scottish Office. As the debates over the 1976 Crofting Act demonstrated, however, there was little appetite in St Andrew's House for radical land reform beyond the limited benefits for crofters, notably the right to share in development value, which that legislation conferred.

The debate which took place in the 1970s remains highly relevant today. Essentially, the arguments about mixing tenure with owner-occupation and croft land with de-crofted land are essentially the same. But the need to make decisions about the direction, and indeed existence, of crofting tenure are now much more urgent. Crofting, as a form of subsistence agriculture usually dependent on ancillary employment, has weakened substantially during the intervening period. Part of that erosion has come from natural demographic change; part from increased prosperity combined with low agricultural prices – which make the efforts that go into crofting even more disproportionate than before to the returns. But another major contributory factor has been the development of a de facto market in crofts which pays little or no heed to the crofting or community interest. Virtually every township has been adversely affected, in crofting terms, by the impact of that market and the infrequency of intervention by the Crofters Commission.

There is a well-worn aphorism about crofts being small pieces of land surrounded by regulations. But that definition contains a necessary truth. The economy within which we all live is largely run on market principles. Being lively and creative creatures, markets will always try to intrude on any territory from which they are excluded. Therefore, if any sector of our economy is to be excluded from the market, then the defences had better be pretty tight – or else the market will gain entry. The idea that there is a convenient half-way house – in which the virtues of crofting tenure are retained but the property market is allowed to operate – remains a delusion which leads logically to the demise of a good system. ●

South Lochs, Western Isles

Cailean Maclean

Torrin, Isle of Skye with Blaven in
the background

Crofting People and Politics

4. ON THE SHOULDERS OF GIANTS

Crofting in the 1980s
Torcuil Crichton

Torcuil Crichton is the son of the late John Crichton, whose involvement in crofting affairs spanned the Federation of Crofters Unions and the Scottish Crofters Union. Born in Swordale, Lewis, he started in journalism with the West Highland Free Press in 1987 spending much of his time continuing the paper's traditions of campaigning against landlordism and for land reform. He now reports internationally for the Sunday Herald newspaper and is a regular contributor in Gaelic and English to BBC radio.

From the distance of twenty years – Live 8 to Live Aid if you want – the 1980s belong to another epoch. At the beginning of that decade the concept of the global village, a planet constantly linked by satellite television, mobile phone and e-mail, was in the realms of science fiction. The Highland village extended as far as the peat banks, because people still cut peat for fuel, and the limits of the common grazings. The ambitions of crofting did not extend much further.

By the time the 1980s came to an end we knew about famine and land evictions in the the Highlands of Ethiopia, the same political forces that had played through parts of the Scottish Highlands a century earlier. Our world, through the forces of technology, global capitalism and interdependent politics was changing rapidly. And, strange as it might seem, crofting, a century old system of land tenure, finished the decade as as a model for sustainable land use across Europe.

Britain, where articles like this were clacked out on typewriters (remember them), emerged battered from the 1970s and the politics had swung to the right with the election of a Conservative government under Margaret Thatcher.

For better or worse Thatcherism defined the decade with monetarist policies that rolled back the state, undermined trade unions, and gave primacy to individual acquisition. Inordinate imbalances of wealth and poverty were created during a painful transition from industrial to a consumer society.

In these parts of the UK that had not endorsed the Tories, primarily Scotland and Wales, the political class felt they were under the heel of an occupying power. As local authorities found services squeezed to the pips, and the police drew their truncheons against striking miners a remarkable renaissance was taking place in the north of Scotland – a trade union was being reborn.

Against the backdrop of the 1980s its all the more remarkable then that this 'trade union' should represent members participating in a system of land tenure, crofting that was distinctive in its low agricultural output and a reliance on communal co-operation, not to mention an image of being reliant on state subsidy for its continued existence.

Without doubt the formation and the flourishing activity of the Scottish Crofters Union in the mid-1980s saved crofting for that time. Through clever positioning and advocacy crofting was presented as diversifying entrepreneurial activity worthy of support and reward and as a form of environmental stewardship unmatched by large scale agriculturalists.

Crofting's most articulate spokesman was James Hunter, a journalist, author and academic, who made an irresistible political case for the crofting communities and assumed the mantle as the first director of the SCU.

The modern union was raised in 1985 out of the ashes of the old Federation of Crofters Unions and some hard work by Hunter, who prepared a feasibility study, and Angus MacLeod, a Lewisman who was the driving force behind the formation of the organisation.

MacLeod, a former tweed entrepreneur, who had that rare distinction of being someone who became more radical the older he became. MacLeod, already in his sixties, harnessed funding, support and agreement across the crofting counties for the initiative with admirable urgency. Within a year of the old federation being wound down a new union had been formed with branches throughout the Highlands and Islands.

The union drew out some amazingly strong characters.

Angus MacRae, a former forester in Lochcarron, became a second father figure for the union along with honorary president Angus MacLeod.

Along with the two big Angus there was another generation of crofter activists who brought the enthusiasm, intelligence and commitment to the project. Frank Rennie, who was the first president of the union, Angus McHattie and his sister Fiona Mandeville, a full time union official, Iain MacIver who later became factor of the Stornoway Trust, Angus Graham, a radical politician and astute businessman who became the union's insurance broker in the islands. The first executive of the union was completed by two of the original members of the Scottish Crofters Federation, my own father John Crichton from Lewis, and Lawrence Graham. They were quite a team. For these first heady years of the union crofting was lifted on the shoulders of giants.

There was phenomenal support for the union throughout the Highlands and Islands. The structure was part-funded by the HIDB and several local authorities and supported enthusiastically and financially by the members themselves. Soon there were more members of the Scottish Crofters Union than there were of National Union of Miners.

On the ground crofting rumbled on and its political successes were not always matched by an agricultural renaissance.

An Integrated Development Programme for agriculture in the Western Isles kicked off in the early 1980s but brought primarily material benefit to crofting townships rather than a fundamental gear shift in the stewardship of the land.

True, there were a number of reseeding and tree-planting schemes carried out but those were far outnumbered by re-fencing projects. Perhaps more rylock fencing was erected in the Western Isles during the IDP period than divided Germany in the last decade of Soviet Communism.

And there was a flip side to the sudden, easy availability of agricultural machinery when combined with the inevitable rising standard of living and changing lifestyles. The post-war communal interdependence based on the one tractor, one mechanical plough and one trailer in each village began to unravel. With a Massey Ferguson in every tarred driveway a crofter could decide to take his peats home, cut his hay or plant his potatoes at his leisure without the help of his neighbours or the resulting obligation of free labour that the support placed upon him.

At first it was a small shift but one which came to have much greater significance in the present day where crofting villages have to scrabble to justify communal activity in the face of housing developers who argue that crofting, apart from individual pursuit of small holdings, is all but dead in some areas.

A smaller scale Skye Development Programme and the larger scale ADP, Agriculture Development Programme followed on. Signs of a fundamental shift away from agriculture were apparent in the funding system put in place for the ADP which delivered significant rewards for environmental and tourism-based projects. The buzz-word of 'diversification' as the EU encouraged small holders across western Europe to think again of their role as producers of livestock and sought to lever agricultural support away from agricultural production.

There was another, more straightforward explanation for the discernible decline in crofting during the 80s. The summers became wetter and in already marginal arable areas the returns from another flattened hayfield began to become frustratingly slim.

Falling stock prices and the increasing costs of importing feed and hay from the drier east coast began to give the whole enterprise a pessimistic air. Skye, always seen as a reservoir of beef stock, held on but in several areas, particularly the Western Isles, cows became as rare on crofts as domestic hens that were being wiped out by a rampant mink population. Precise meteorological data isn't to hand for the 1980s but the steady stream of flatbed lorries carrying bale after bale of hay across the ferry from Kyle to Kyleakin seemed to indicate that something fundamental had changed in the nature of the crofting system.

This decline in agricultural activity may have been masked by the growing confidence within the crofting communities. Slowly but surely over the previous few years crofting had been re-discovering its radical tradition. The pages of the West Highland Free Press, the milestone 'Making of the Crofting Community' and Iain Fraser Grigor's 'Mightier than a Lord' had claimed history back for the people of the Highlands and that began to have an effect.

The high point of this confident expression came with the centenary of the 1886 Crofters Act with the publication of several books and the opening of As an Fhearan, an exhibition curated by An Lanntair gallery in Stornoway which toured throughout Scotland and as far away as Canada.

On the political stage crofting was making progress too. Against the national tide several friends of the crofting community entered parliament in 1987, notably Calum Macdonald in the Western Isles and Brian Wilson, the campaigning journalist, in Cunninghame North, who had been one of the first to suggest the formation of a new crofters organisation.

The political climate should have been against the Crofting Counties, which never delivered electoral success for the Conservative government, but the union confounded expectations, befriended Tory Ministers who should have been at least sceptical and brought them around the camp fire.

The SCU was also making its voice heard in the corridors of power from Edinburgh to Brussels. A highly persuasive paper on the value for money provided by the Crofter housing grant and loan scheme delivered by the SCU blew apart the myths surrounding croft housing and set the standard for other campaigns the union became involved in.

In parliament Calum Macdonald laid plans for the Crofting Forestry Scheme that would enable communities to profit from tree-planting schemes.

Not everything went the way of the Scottish Crofters Union and its

leadership was given a lesson in going ahead of its membership when the Conservative Ministers were persuaded to consider transferring ownership of Department of Agriculture crofting estates to the tenants.

For the government it was a Highland example of privatising state-owned assets and off-loading an over-bureaucratic function. For its proponents, mainly Jim Hunter and the leadership of the crofters union, it was the first step in fully fledged community ownership of all crofting land. The tenants didn't see it that way. On Raasay and in Staffin in the north of Skye, the estates involved, the crofters asked why they should become their own landlords when through their own government they already were. They could see no advantage of taking on the functions that the civil servants carried out on their behalf.

'Crofting is a system of land tenancy, not a means of a few individuals making a small fortune on land speculation on the backs of their neighbours.'

The estates already in public ownership should be the last to be handed to the community said critics of the proposals. There were plenty privately owned crofting estates where the influence of landlordism still had a pernicious effect that should be in the queue for community ownership first.

In the 1980s the number of people who were actively involved in the land reform movement could probably be fitted into the back of a West Highland Free Press delivery van. The subject, although it drew principled support, was not as fashionable as it now is but towards the end of the 1980s the first breeze of what would become a wind of change in land ownership began to blow across the Highlands.

'The gains made by the Scottish Crofters Union were thrown away by the disastrous choices of its senior officials in the following decade while the power of the environmental lobby has grown untrammelled. But what the union and crofting are about still hold true.'

On the island of Eigg people who had long suffered under the dead hand of landlordism began to find the voice to express their frustration. In the north west, in Assynt, fireside conversation began to turn seriously towards taking crofting land out of the lottery of private landownership with people like Bill Ritchie, another SCU activist, taking a lead role.

By the time the decade came to a close the Scottish Crofters Union was, in the words of its president Angus MacRae, 'part of the furniture', just as he wanted it. Though intense activity, firm campaigning and some inspired leadership it had managed to rejuvenate the image and status of crofting and throw up a whole generation of activists. Crofters, because of the demands of their work and the marginal nature of their land, could always walk the walk. With the SCU they could now talk the talk too.

> Crofting today: Hands that have not sheared a sheep in twenty years and been rendered soft by padding a keyboard should not perhaps sit in judgement on the future of crofting.

On the surface crofting continues to have less active participants than in the past. In some villages horses are more plentiful than sheep but there are occasional encouraging signs. Cows, for example, have begun to appear again in Lewis villages.

The gains made by the Scottish Crofters Union were thrown away by the disastrous choices of its senior officials in the following decade while the power of the environmental lobby has grown untrammelled. But what the union and crofting are about still hold true.

The Lochcarron forester and crofter, the late Angus MacRae, a sage and wise man, always maintained that agricultural activity had to remain central to crofting. Nowadays that statement contains something of a paradox. The modern argument for crofting has to be presented on environmental and social grounds. A simple agricultural defence will not withstand the whirlwind of reform that will one day come to the Common Agricultural Policy. Given that 80% of agricultural subsidy goes to only 20%

of European farmers it should be possible to carry out reform without destroying small scale agriculture but to ensure that is the case a sustainable argument for crofting has to be made all over again.

Rocketing land prices are already putting incredible pressure on Highland communities as more and more land is taken out of crofting use for speculative housing development. Crofting is a system of land tenancy, not a means of a few individuals making a small fortune on land speculation on the backs of their neighbours. The law should be framed and exercised with this, and MacRae's rule of the primacy of agricultural activity, in mind.

The ugly spectacle of the current land grab by individual crofters is a result of sudden increase in land value and an accompanying decline in communal dependence, something which first became apparent with the increasing individual wealth in the 1980s.

The next monetary cloud on the horizon is the new energy boom and the implications it might have for consensus within crofting communities. Many areas stand to benefit from wind farm developments with annual payments to community managed funds from farm operators. However, the whole system of profit-sharing and communal agreement to development is already being undermined by individual crofters demanding their share of profits upfront. Crofting was never profitable but with rocketing land prices being a crofter is. The challenge is to prevent the race for profits destroying the crofting system itself. •

Crofting People and Politics

5. HISTORY WILL JUDGE

The 1990s
David Ross

David Ross has been Highland Correspondent of The Herald since 1988. Brought up in Perthshire and Argyll, his mother's people were, and still are, crofters on Iona where he spent virtually every holiday trying to learn the skills of haymaking and elementary husbandry. After studying history at Edinburgh University he worked for nine years as a staff journalist on the Times Educational Supplement Scotland before joining The Herald.

On Saturday the 14th September 1991 a plaque was unveiled on top of a cairn at Inverie in Knoydart. It commemorated the seven local men, including the priest, who in 1948 staged the penultimate land raid in the Scottish Highlands. They had occupied a number of fields on the Knoydart estate, which at that time was owned by the former Nazi sympathiser Lord Brocket. The seven proceeded to peg out a number of crofts for themselves.

The crofts were their units of hope; the only mechanism to secure a future for the themselves on their people's land. The plaque bore the legend:

> 'Justice! In 1948 near the cairn, Seven Men of Knoydart staked claims to secure a place to live and work. For over a century Highlanders had been forced to use land raids to gain a foothold where their forebears lived. Their struggle should inspire each new generation of Scots to gain such rights by just laws. History will judge harshly the oppressive laws that have led to the virtual extinction of a unique culture from this beautiful place.'

The 1948 raid was to fail, not least because of a lack of government will. Neither did it have any positive legacy for the people of Knoydart. The estate was to be progressively split up and sold off, often to highly inappropriate parties. One by one the people left until today there is not a single resident who can claim to be truly local.

But nonetheless, that day in 1991 was a symbolic occasion, and in more ways than one. For those who knew and cared about the Knoydart raiders and what their cause represented, it was appropriate and poignant that they be remembered in this way. To those with a different perspective

'The crofts were their units of hope; the only mechanism to secure a future for themselves on their people's land. . . For those who knew and cared about the Knoydart raiders and what their cause represented, it was appropriate and poignant that they be remembered in this way.'

on the human story of the Highlands and Islands, it was also appropriate – fine words in an out-of-the-way place serving a silly cause pursued by those who somehow dreamed of reversing the nineteenth century clearances – an utter irrelevance to contemporary Scotland.

The former firmly believed that the only reason there was anything of social worth left in the Highlands and islands in the late twentieth century was due entirely to the continuation of the crofting system. This and this alone had allowed the survival of the Gaels' intrinsic sense of their place.

This view was to be supported by research by Dr Gordon MacMillan of Edinburgh University who was commissioned by the Crofters Commission in 1996 to evaluate crofting as a tool to help maintain the welfare of rural population in marginal areas.

As part of that study a comparison was done between the experience of non-crofting and crofting areas such as Cabrach in upland Grampian seventeen miles south west of Huntly and outwith the crofting area; and Rogart in the crofting county of Sutherland. Although life would have been broadly similar, the study found:

'Over the past century the total population of Rogart has fallen by 63% from 1,227 to 450; while in Cabrach it has fallen by a staggering 87% from 646 in 1891 to a contemporary population of only 80.'

More generally the report concluded :

'It is remarkable that any Gaelic culture has survived the considerable social upheavals and sustained depopulation that the Highlands and Islands have experienced. Even though the most significant transformations had occurred before crofting legislation was implemented, it is likely that the region's cultural heritage would be even more seriously undermined if legislation had never existed at all. The most significant observation is that the ties between individual people and particular places lie at the root of Gaelic and Norse cultures, and crofting legislation has played a crucial role

Crofting People and Politics

in maintaining that union over the past century. Even though large numbers of households have left, the families that remain on crofts still occupy land that has a cultural as well as economic significance to them.'

However others believed with equal conviction that the crofting system as established by the Crofting Act of 1886, and further regulated by later legislation, had served only to lower the ambition and reduce opportunities of a quasi-peasant community which was trapped in a pernicious and debilitating dependency culture.

The backcloth was a continuing debate about the clearances, their twentieth century legacy, the lasting power of the landlord. A debate which had become quite sterile. But things were beginning to move further north.

In 1991 the Scottish Land Court found in favour of a sacked worker from the Kinlochewe Estate in Ross-shire who was seeking a house site on croftland. The force of this decision, subsequently upheld by the Court of Session, was that no longer could a landlord expect half the value of any development on a croft which was being bought by a crofter under the right-to-buy established in the 1976 Crofting Act, and then decrofting it. Crofters could buy their crofts and then pass them to a local crofting trust without the landlord receiving any more than fifteen times the annual rent. It was to prove timely.

In the spring and early summer of 1992 it emerged that the owners of the 21,500 acre North Lochinver Estate were bankrupt and forced to sell their land. Scandinavian Property Services (SPS) Ltd had bought the estate in three lots in 1989 from the Vestey family for £1,080,000. What its development plans were for the area remain unclear as does the level of their knowledge of the restrictions that went with land which was 95% under crofting tenure. But SPS's main creditors, the Ostgota Enskilda Bank of Stockholm wanted as much of their money back as possible and liquidators, Stoy Hayward of London, decided to put the North Lochinver estate on the market in seven different lots but with a guide price for the total of £473,000.

'. . . the only reason there was anything of social worth left in the Highlands and Islands in the late twentieth century was due entirely to the continuation of the crofting system. This and this alone had allowed the survival of the Gaels' intrinsic sense of place.'

The 100 local crofters were deeply alarmed by the prospect of a fragmentation of ownership which could leave them dealing with several different landlords and divided common grazings. But the sales particulars also promoted the idea of wilderness, which did little to ease the crofters' concerns.

A special meeting of the Assynt Branch of the Scottish Crofters Union was called on June 6. They met in Stoer hall, and three days later issued a public statement declaring their '. . . anger and determination to resist the attempted sale in small lots of part of the former Assynt estate.'

At that point they had only agreed to pursue the possibility of establishing a trust to purchase the land. But they also made clear they were looking to government agencies and local authorities in the

Crofting People and Politics

Highlands and Islands to '. . . seize this opportunity to demonstrate their concern and support for crofting.'

It was the effective launch of a campaign which was to strik e a chord throughout the land. Ever since the industrial revolutions of Europe and North America the urbanised populations have often displayed an ambivalence to those who stayed in the rural areas. There is often a negative, patronising element in this. But every so often there is a different perspective on the countryside and its history; that they hold some kind of national truth, a set of fundamental values, that are still relevant to modern life. The response to the Assynt story appeared to confirm this as men and women across the land queued up to seize this opportunity to demonstrate their concern and support.

After their initial attempts to buy were rebuffed the crofters threatened to deploy the 1976 right to buy. This provision had been criticised by many, including this writer, as a threat to the integrity of the crofting community, but it helped do the trick in Assynt. If the sellers weren't going to sell to them, they would make the property unsellable to anyone else.

The Assynt Crofters' success was trumpeted across the land. Although crofters on the Stornoway Trust had been running their own affairs for decades, the £300,000 purchase in Assynt was seen to show that progress on the land question was possible; that there was a middle way between land nationalisation and landlordism.

Within the year a far quieter buyout was underway on Skye where the twenty crofters in the townships of Borve and Annishader bought their 4,500 acres at the suggestion of Major John Macdonald, the owner of the Skeabost estate. This was after he and the crofters had failed to reach an agreement for a project under the 1991 Crofter Forestry Act.

There had been a tradition of good relations on the estate. Major Macdonald's grandfather Lachlan Macdonald took over Skeabost in 1874. Reputed to be the richest man in Skye, he cancelled all rent arrears and allowed his tenants to fix their own rents, which had remained largely unchanged. But the people of Borve and Annishader believed their community needed more than just low rents for the twenty first century.

It seemed to be catching. The Crofters at Melness were offered control of the 11,000 acres by their Nottinghamshire-based landlord Michael Foljamble. Others followed.

There appeared to be a new optimism about crofting, which had been sustained by the Scottish Crofters Union in the late 1980s and early 90s. But signals from government were confusing. Lord James Douglas Hamilton was happy to praise the Assynt crofters and earlier Lord Sanderson of Bowden had offered to hand over the running of the publicly owned crofting estates in Skye and Raasay to their tenants in a pilot project.

This was followed by Michael Forsyth, the Secretary of State, who had started his very public love affair with the Highlands and Islands in 1995, by launching his proposal to hand over control of all the publicly owned crofting estates to local crofting trusts. But he also exhorted private landlords to follow his example, thereby implicitly suggesting that either the local community had more right to the land, or would make better use of it.

He was said to have been impressed by arguments advanced by Dr Jim Hunter, the former director of the Scottish Crofters Union and the leading historian of crofting (a fellow essayist in this book) who has been an outstanding advocate of crofting and the Highlands and Islands' interests for the past two decades. The two had a private meeting at Sabhal Mòr Ostaig the day the Skye Bridge opened in 1995 when Hunter is known to have promoted increased community management of publicly owned crofting estates and Forestry Commission land.

But behind the scenes things were a little different. In 1996, under pressure from a Treasury review, the Scottish Office had proposed the replacement of the Crofting Counties Agricultural Grants Scheme (CCAGS) with the Scottish Countryside Premium Scheme (SCPS) At that time CCAGS disbursed about £3m a year to crofters, but the SCPS was a Scotland-wide scheme which would have left crofters competing with the nation's farmers for a share of £7m.

At the same time it was proposed that the loan element of Crofting Building Grants and Loans Scheme (CBGLS), which accounted for more than half the money spent under the Scheme, was to be dropped, leaving crofters to raise the balance commercially. It emerged that Sir Hector Munro, as agriculture minister and Ian Lang as secretary of state, had resisted this very proposal two years earlier, arguing it would not be wise to 'stir up crofting matters' for what would be a small saving in the £5m scheme. Ironically it was only to prove politically possible to withdraw the loan element within the last year and under a Scottish Parliament.

'The future of crofting had become inextricably linked with the cause of land reform, whose momentum was unstoppable by the late 1990s.'

In 1996 there was unanimity of informed opinion that the proposed changes in CCAGS and CBGLS could be the final nail in crofting's coffin. The Commission told Mr Forsyth with uncharacteristic frankness that the demise of CCAGS would mean three out of four working crofters would be significantly worse off, that the new-found confidence in crofting would be destroyed, dereliction and depopulation would follow. The Scottish Crofters Union warned that the removal of the loan element from CBGLS would make it almost impossible for many crofters to raise the necessary money to build their houses.

The proposals would have saved the Treasury money and would have undermined crofting's perceived dependency culture. Goals that Michael Forsyth could have been expected to enthusiastically support given his earlier embrace of Thatcherism. But at the Scottish Grand Committee meeting in Dundee in May of 1996 Mr Forsyth unashamedly publicly dumped both.

The next big community buyout was the island of Eigg where the long time owner Keith Schellenberg had succeeded in finding a laird in his own controversial mould – the German 'fire artist' Maruma. The subsequent complex financial saga rendered the island the plaything of international land speculators, and ended in court. Inspired by Assynt and Borve and Annishader, the community mounted a successful buyout, facilitated by an anonymous English benefactress.

The crofting community on Eigg was small and so the buyout was not influenced by crofting laws. But the cause of land reform was further advanced the day the islanders took over, along with their partners the Highlands Council and the Scottish Wildlife Trust.

By this time a Labour government had been returned with a huge majority and on June 12 1997 Brian Wilson, a new minister of state at the Scottish Office arrived in Eigg to join the celebrations and to announce that he had given instructions to Highlands and Islands Enterprise to assist initiatives to achieve community ownership. This was to pave the way for the establishment of the Scottish Land Fund two years later with an initial budget of £10m, which was to support a range of community buyouts, not least the £1.6m which went to help buy the croftland on the 55,000 acre North Harris Estate.

Mr Wilson had campaigned for land reform for most of his adult life and had outraged landowners across the Highlands and Islands for his withering attacks on their interests largely through the pages of the West Highland Free Press, which he had helped found twenty five years earlier.

Mr Wilson said there should have been a community-led buy out of the island decades ago, but it had been frustrated.

> 'Over the past 30 years, stewardship of this island has come to symbolise much that was wrong about the free market and land. The challenge now for everyone involved in this great undertaking is to create a symbol of hope and achievement which others will be inspired to follow.'

The future of crofting had become inextricably linked with the cause of land reform, whose momentum was unstoppable by the late 1990s. In the final year of the decade the Scottish Executive made a most significant announcement. Subject to ministerial assent, and local democratic approval, crofting communities would have an absolute right to buy their land whether or not the owner wished to sell. Opponents compared it to the government-backed land grabs in Zimbabwe.

But Brian Wilson, by then a minister at the newly created Scotland Office, saw it differently:

> 'It is by far the most radical aspect of the whole package and a deep gloom would have been cast over many communities if the prize had been lost at this stage.
>
> 'You only have to look at Uig in Lewis to see the contrast where the

'It does seem odd that just a few years after having held their political nerve over the crofting community's right to buy, facing down comparisons with Robert Mugabe and claims of human rights denials, that ministers should take their eye off the crofting ball.'

Bhaltos estate is now community owned and is now bristling with ideas and potential, while next door there is 40,000 acres of sheer absentee-owned dereliction. That is what can now change as of right and it will be the finest thing to happen in the Highlands and Islands since the Crofting Act of 1886.'

Non-crofting communities would only enjoy a right of pre-emption if and when any landowner decided to sell. But the needs and aspirations of crofting communities were to be recognised with a special place within the law of the land, before the interests of the landlords. It was something which couldn't have been anticipated eight year's earlier by those at the cairn at Inverie, and simply couldn't have been imagined by those they were commemorating.

But whither now for crofting and our 18,000 crofts? More will be created but there are grave concerns despite the progress made in the 1990s. Ironically there are fears the new Crofting Reform Bill could yet undermine the system by failing to control the growing market in assignations, indeed that it may encourage the development of one.

It does seem odd that just a few years after having held their political nerve over the crofting community's right to buy, facing down comparisons with Robert Mugabe and claims of human rights denials, that ministers should take their eye off the crofting ball.

But as this article was being written it was evident that ministers were aware of these concerns. One avenue which should be explored is that on community-owned land at least the local crofters' trust assumes a quasi-regulatory role locally on contentious issues of assignation and absenteeism, with the Crofters Commission or Scottish Land Court acting as a court of appeal.

The trusts have democratic credentials for such a job. In addition given a crofting community buyout can only be undertaken with majority local support, it may be that the 1976 right to buy their own croft on such land should be withdrawn. It sits uneasily with the new powers which give crofting communities the right to realise their ambitions, normally with the support of public and lottery money, yet leave these plans open to sabotage by one or two malcontents.

If the landlord is powerless to resist local democratically-backed moves for community buyouts, should individual crofters retain a legal right to opt out? The right to buy never had anything to do with security of tenure. That issue was settled a very long time before.

If such community-owned, self-regulating estates were to become widespread, crofting could help shape Scotland in the twenty first century. That should be crofting's goal. •

Crofting People and Politics

6. MARKING FIFTY YEARS OF THE CROFTERS COMMISSION

The crofting future

James Hunter

Professor James Hunter heads the University of the Highlands and Islands Centre for History at Dornoch. A former Chair of Highlands and Islands Enterprise, he helped organise the Scottish Crofters Union (now the Scottish Crofting Foundation) and became the organisation's first director. He is the author of two books about the development of crofting – and has written widely on the history of the Highlands and Islands.

In the run-up to the organisation's fiftieth birthday, the Crofters Commission organised a seminar on crofting prospects. Most of the gathering's participants were crofters and, though they took the opportunity to air a number of grievances, their overall stance was strikingly optimistic. Crofting, seminar participants concluded, could readily have 'a positive future'. The Scottish Executive's Crofting (Reform) Bill, they went on, should embody a vision of this future and should be clear, too, as to the many developmental, social, cultural, agricultural and environmental benefits which an ambitious and forward-looking policy for crofting could offer Scotland as a whole.

This verdict may have owed something to the setting in which it was reached. The commission's seminar took place at Sabhal Mòr Ostaig on Skye's Sleat peninsula. Scotland's crofting localities contain few more inspiring institutions. At Sabhal Mòr, launched thirty years ago in the then crumbling remnants of one of the farm steadings put up in the aftermath of the Highland Clearances, degree-level courses are taught – through the medium of Gaelic – in architecturally spectacular buildings which, if all goes to plan, will shortly be part of a fully-fledged University of the Highlands and Islands. Because Sabhal Mòr provides 70-plus good jobs and because the college attracts hundreds of students, the crofting townships in its vicinity have been transformed. Sleat, once the most run-down corner of a badly run-down island, now contains lots of new residents – many of them occupying prosperous-looking homes.

Much the same is true of the rest of Skye. In recent decades, the island's population, which previously fell steadily for more than 120 years, has grown by nearly 50 per cent – and to be able to remember a time when

Skye had more inhabitants than it has in 2005 you would need today to be more than 90 years of age.

Given that I have been asked to look fifty years into the future, it is salutary to begin by underlining the fact that no-one forecast Skye's population growth before it occurred. Of equal significance in the present context is the further fact that, in the course of the two centuries which have passed since crofts as we know them first took shape, there have been few periods prior to the present when knowledgeable observers would have bet heavily, or at all, on crofting's long-run survival.

If a gathering of the sort the Crofters Commission organised at Sabhal Mòr Ostaig had been held in Sleat 150 years ago, its assessment of crofting's future would have been inescapably and unremittingly bleak. Skye in 1855 had experienced nearly a decade of famine. Dozens of crofting townships were being emptied to make way for sheep. The island's remaining crofting families lived in tumbledown hovels and in the sort of desperate poverty not to be found in our time outside the most deprived parts of sub-Saharan Africa. Men, women and children usually wore only rags. Household possessions commonly consisted of nothing other than than one or two worn-out blankets, a cooking pot and a couple of spoons. One charitable body organised regular handouts of oatmeal. Another helped ship hundreds of Skye folk to Australia. There they were subjected to treatment of the sort that so-called asylum-seekers commonly receive today.

Anyone reaching Melbourne from Skye or elsewhere in the Highlands and Islands was routinely categorised as 'indolent' or 'dirty'.

'I am put to great difficulty with these people,' an Australian immigration official commented of one refugee contingent, 'because I am unable to communicate with them except by signs. . . I do not understand one word of Gaelic, and they do not understand one word of English.' Much the most unattractive thing about families from the north of

Scotland, the same man went on, was 'the uncleanliness of their habits'. Highlanders and Hebrideans, he wrote, were 'as near an approach to barbarians as any [immigrants] I have ever met with.'

A century later, in 1955, Skye's crofting communities were doing better. But the population outflow which had begun more than a hundred years before was, if anything, accelerating. Hence the gloomy note struck by a government-appointed Commission of Enquiry into Crofting Conditions when it reported in 1954. 'It must be said,' commission members observed, 'that our survey of the crofting system leaves one dominant impression in our minds. It is a system which, as now organised, is fighting a losing battle against the social and economic forces of the day. In many places. . . it is in a state of decline and in some, indeed, of dissolution.'

As is clear from such comments, the Crofters Commission, which was set up in 1955 to give effect to the enquiry commission's reform proposals, faced a daunting task. Reporting that same year on the outcome of his painstaking analysis of demographic trends in the West Highlands and Islands, the pioneer ecologist, Frank Fraser Darling, noted of Skye:

> '[Population] decline has continued without a break since 1841. . . The rate of decline in 1931-51 was high. . . In Sleat the population is down to a fifth of its maximum. Since 1931 [the population of] Kilmuir and Duirinish has been reduced by one-quarter. . . Further decline in the population is inevitable.'

This was especially disappointing because of the high hopes for crofting engendered in Skye by the island's role in successive campaigns for land reform. During the 1880s, Skye was in the vanguard of the land seizures and rent-strikes which enabled the Highland Land League to win the security of tenure delivered by the Crofters Act of 1886. At the start of the twentieth century, the island was convulsed by a further round of land raids which led to the greater part of Skye passing into public ownership,

Affordable housing on former common grazing land, Shieldaig, Wester Ross

the demise of most of the big farms created in the course of the clearances and the establishment – on former farms – of hundreds of new crofts.

Like other crofts, however, these new holdings typically ran to no more than a few acres of arable. This meant that their occupants could not earn a livelihood from their agricultural efforts alone. Crofters needed other jobs. And whether in Skye or in the rest of the crofting area, between the 1920s and the 1960s, worthwhile jobs were hard to find. Everywhere in the Highlands and Islands, local economies were contracting and people – young people in particular – left each year in huge numbers. Many crofts were tenanted, if they were tenanted at all, by absentees. Hundreds more holdings were vacant – for the reason that, though they could have been got for the asking, nobody wanted them.

Soft fruit and vegetable production on a croft in Shetland

The crofting situation in which the Crofters Commission took shape, then, was the reverse of the situation which the Commission confronts today. Where once population loss seemed endemic and unstoppable, it has given way – in Skye and in lots of other places – to in-migration on a substantial scale. Where once there were no tenants for crofts, there is now overwhelming demand for them. Where once croft tenancies changed hands for nothing or next to nothing, they now sell for large sums. And where once it was extremely hard to connect crofting requirements with national policy objectives, now it is comparatively straightforward. 'With the shift away from production-led agricultural support,' as was concluded by the Crofters Commission seminar mentioned previously, 'the case for crofting can be made in a much more positive and upbeat fashion than was possible in the past.'

'. . . a well-populated countryside which sustains a diverse economy, attracts visitors, conserves natural habitats, safeguards distinctive cultures and fosters organically-produced niche crops as well as force-fed monocultures. This is exactly what crofting has offered, still offers – and, given the opportunity, could offer more widely.'

Given those unprecedented – and, in many respects, heartening – circumstances, the Scottish Executive's Crofting (Reform) Bill ought arguably to have been preceded by a root-and-branch review of how crofting might most constructively be taken forward. This was what happened in the past. The 1886 Crofters Act was preceded by a royal commission. The 1955 Act – which brought the present-day Crofters Commission into existence – was the outcome, as already indicated, of a similar enquiry process. And the comprehensive reports resulting from those efforts – the first published in 1884, the second seventy years later – leave no doubt as to the seriousness with which the British governments of the 1880s and 1950s took crofting.

It is hard, on the basis of the available evidence, to believe that the Scottish Executive attaches the same importance to this same topic. The enquiry reports of 1884 and 1954 are thoughtful, carefully considered and sometimes moving documents. Here, for instance, is the 1954 commission of enquiry on why crofting communities, for all their numerical insignificance, merit attention from Britain's legislators:

> 'The terms of our remit presuppose that it is desirable to maintain a smallholding population in the Highlands and Islands, and it is therefore unnecessary for us to argue the case in favour of that proposition. We have thought it right, however, to record our unanimous conviction, founded on personal knowledge and on the evidence we have received, that in the national interest the maintenance of these communities is desirable because they embody a free and independent way of life which, in a civilisation predominantly urban and industrial in character, is worth preserving for its own intrinsic quality.'

You will search in vain among the documentation which the Executive has produced in support of its Crofting Bill for any equivalent statement. Far from dealing in visionary language of the kind deployed by the enquiry team of fifty years back, the Scottish Executive's published accounts of its crofting policies are couched in management-speak of a sort that seems intended to preclude the possibility of crofting being approached in ways that capitalise far-sightedly on what this smallholding system, or some modified version of it, could contribute to the regeneration not just of the Highlands and Islands but of the wider Scottish countryside.

This is all the more lamentable because, as was stressed at the Crofters Commission's fiftieth-anniversary seminar, the case for crofting is currently more persuasive than it has ever been before. For all its eloquence, the 1954 commission of enquiry had to engage continually in special pleading because it operated in a policy climate that was deeply inimical to crofting; a climate in which national policy was geared to maximising food output and, in consequence, to promoting big farms at the expense of small; a climate which gave no priority to the natural environment and regarded rural depopulation as the inevitable concomitant of agricultural advance.

Today, in contrast, rural policy – both at the United Kingdom and European Union level – is meant to deliver a whole set of objectives. Success is no longer defined in terms of intensive food production. What is wanted, we are told, is a well-populated countryside which sustains a diverse economy, attracts visitors, conserves natural habitats, safeguards distinctive cultures and fosters organically-produced niche crops as well as force-fed monocultures.

This is exactly what crofting has offered, still offers – and, given the opportunity, could offer more widely. It is from this point that a genuinely creative strategy for crofting would start. Such a strategy – rather than becoming bogged down, as the Crofting (Reform) Bill does so depressingly and so mind-numbingly, in legalistic minutiae – would attempt to identify, perhaps by means of a full-scale and on-the-ground enquiry of the 1954 type, what needs to be done to enable crofting both to capitalise on its potential and to break out of the legislative laager to which the Crofting Bill is so anxious to confine it.

How might we create in semi-deserted Perthshire glens and long-

'How might we create in semi-deserted Perthshire glens and long depopulated Borders valleys, where neither hill farms nor forestry provide worthwhile employment opportunities, flourishing communities of the type to be seen in Sleat? By what means could new crofts be created on a really big scale in areas where demand for them is becoming insatiable? Why are we not promoting forest-based smallholdings on the Scandinavian pattern?'

depopulated Borders valleys, where neither hill farms nor plantation forestry provide worthwhile employment opportunities, flourishing communities of the type to be seen in Sleat? By what means could new crofts be created on a really big scale in areas where demand for them is becoming insatiable? Why are we not promoting forest-based smallholdings on the Scandinavian pattern? Might crofting be managed and expanded in ways that do not involve the Crofting Bill's ceaseless recourse to legal mechanisms of indefensible complexity and cost?

These and a thousand other questions ought to be asked and answered before crofting reform goes ahead. Sadly, however, the consultative process surrounding the Scottish Parliament's first stab at crofting legislation has been so off-puttingly technical and constrained as to ensure

Crofting People and Politics

that most such issues, where touched on at all, have been mentioned only to be dismissed.

The Crofters Commission, to its great credit, has recently been responding to changing circumstances by interpreting its remit as creatively and constructively as possible. Hence, for example, the appearance of the first new crofts seen in a generation. Initiatives of this type have both been facilitated by, and have helped underpin, the Scottish Executive's land reform agenda – an agenda which is one of the Executive's real success stories and an agenda which should have resulted in MSPs being invited to grapple every bit as energetically with crofting possibilities as they did with the concept of community ownership.

The Crofting Future

Think about what land reform of the sort promoted by the Executive and embraced by the Parliament has done for an island like Gigha – where, after just three years of community ownership, population has shot up, homes have been built and refurbished, businesses established, employment generated and a locally-controlled windfarm brought into production. This is the sort of dynamism which, if the Executive stopped treating crofting reform as an administrative chore and began thinking about it as a political opportunity, a re-energised crofting system could readily play into.

Crofting has survived much worse than the Scottish Executive's Crofting (Reform) Bill as drafted. That is why, irrespective of the Bill's final form, crofts and crofters will still be around in 2055. But both crofters and crofts will be more plentiful and more prosperous in fifty years time if the chance is taken to make today's Crofting Bill a milestone of the kind put in place in 1955 and, still more, in 1886.

In the present Executive, not least in the present First Minister, the Highlands and Islands have good friends – people who have engaged productively with the case for a Highlands and Islands University, the case for public sector jobs dispersal, the case for land reform. It is not to be over-optimistic about the future to anticipate equally positive engagement with the case for crofting. •

'the talk was of crofting's role in rural affairs as one model of development which more than ever has potential to sustain communities and cultures. It will require that we continue striving for active croft use with quality products; and that we accelerate the creation of new crofts, made easier by the new Crofting Bill, to give a secure home and business base in fragile communities.'

David Green, Chairman's Foreword
Crofters Commission Annual Report 2005

Cailean Maclean

Peat Stack, South Uist

Clerk, Skye grazings

Stacking peats, 1950s

Caílean Maclean

Crofts at Drumfearn, Skye

'Crofting already supports more people to the acre, so to speak, than any other non-urban land use currently available in Scotland; more than hill farming; more than commercial forestry, the type which expanded so massively in the course of the 1970s and 1980s; more than deer forest or grouse moor. Where the occupants of those part-time holdings which remain characteristic of most crofting localities have access to additional sources of income, then crofting can readily constitute the basis of a very satisfactory way of living.'

from *The Claim of Crofting*
by James Hunter
(Mainstream Publishing) 1991

Crofters Commisssion Board Members 2005

(l to r) Robin Currie, Roderick Murray, Isobel MacPhail,
David Green, Drew Ratter, Sarah Allen and Andrew Thin